A Land

'The Land Army fights in the fields. It is in the fields of Britain that the most critical battle of the present war may well be fought and won.'

Lady Denman
Director of the Women's Land Army

A Land Girl's War

Joan Snelling

Old Pond Publishing

First published 2004

Reprinted 2007

Copyright © Joan Snelling, 2004
The moral right of the author has been asserted

All rights reserved. No parts of this publication may be
reproduced, stored in a retrieval system, or transmitted, in
any form or by any means electronic, mechanical,
photocopying, recording or otherwise, without prior
permission of Old Pond Publishing.

ISBN 978 1 903366 67 7

A catalogue record for this book is available from the
British Library

Published by
Old Pond Publishing
Dencora Business Centre
36 Whitehouse Road
Ipswich IP1 5LT
United Kingdom
www.oldpond.com

Cover design by Liz Whatling
Printed and bound in Great Britain by
Biddles Ltd, King's Lynn
Typeset by Galleon Typesetting, Ipswich

Contents

*Dedicated to the memory of my
many friends who died during the
Second World War, 1939–1945*

The War Begins

I AM peeling carrots at the kitchen sink. Nothing unusual about that, but for the past sixty years, every time I do this job, my mind goes straight back to my first day as a farm labourer. It was in April 1941 and there were an awful lot of carrots, at least five acres of them. Because this was fiddling work, the local gang of women casual workers had been called in. We had to pick up the carrots as they were ploughed out, rub off any soil and put them into net sacks.

There were also the six Land Army girls who were already employed on the farm before I arrived. The carrots were all shapes and sizes and some looked rather rude, as carrots do sometimes. This was the delight of the village women, who roared with laughter and made suggestive remarks and waved the carrots around, looking at us girls to see how we were taking it, especially at me, the newest recruit and a bit shy. Laughter is infectious and it was all good humoured and when the long back-breaking day's work finally ended, I pedalled my bike wearily the eight miles home.

Only it wasn't really home, just a temporary wartime one. My real home was in London, but our family were on holiday in Norfolk when the Prime Minister declared war with Germany on the radio on 3 September 1939. This was a solemn moment which had been expected for some time, but it was still a bitter blow when it finally happened and all England was listening in silence and wondering just what to expect. Afterwards I went down the garden to the river and cried sadly. My friend Bill was a bomber pilot and he had said that if there was a war, he would be amongst the first to be 'bumped off'. And so he was, just six months later in 1940, on a night reconnaissance flight over France, one of the first amongst the thousands who would die during the next six years.

Our family split up. Londoners had been warned to expect bombing raids and it was wiser to stay in the country if one could. Our holiday home was rented and its owner wanted to move back in again after the summer. So we looked around Ludham to find something else. There wasn't much choice and my mother was lucky to find a bungalow which she agreed to rent from a local blacksmith for an indefinite period. Everyone said that the war would be over by Christmas. It wasn't, of course, and six years later we were still there.

It was decided that my mother, myself, my sister-in-law and her small baby should stay in Ludham for safety. My brother volunteered for the Army soon after. My father went back to London to work, where he would live in my brother's house in the suburbs, with our cook to look after him. Our housemaid went off to do war work, and so we were all scattered.

The move to the bungalow was in three stages. Mother went first in the car, driven by our chauffeur, taking what little luggage we had, which was all summer holiday clothes. I followed on my bike and Babe, my sister-in-law, came last, pushing Margaret in her pram and accompanied by our wire-haired terrier on his lead.

Hillview, furnished with plain 1930s furniture, was neither large nor beautiful. A square block, it contained two bedrooms which were allotted to my mother and Babe, and there was a small sitting room, kitchen and bathroom. There was a large roof space above, with a dormer window and access by a ladder from the kitchen. This became my abode. It was spacious, though sparsely furnished, and I only fell down the ladder once in six years.

The cold water tank was in my attic. Water had to be pumped up to it by hand, from a pump in the garden. This was hard work as it took several hundred pumps to fill the tank.

I was seventeen in 1939 and old enough to learn to drive. The chauffeur had taken Mother's car to London, where it was put up on bricks and generally prepared for a long stay in its garage. Then he went off to join the Army. My brother's car was at Hillview and I had a provisional licence, so a girlfriend gave me my one and only driving lesson in this, during which the gear lever came off in my hand. Then petrol was rationed and that was the end of unnecessary journeys and my lessons. Only people doing essential work were given a petrol allowance.

I still had my bike, which I had hired every summer holiday since I was twelve, so we bought it from the garage, together with another one for Babe. Hers was painted dull matt black, so we called it Deadly Nightshade. Mine was Nausea Bagwash, after a character in a radio comedy. I painted both names on the mudguards.

Babe was so-called because she was the youngest of a large family. It was a bit hard on her, having to live with her in-laws with her husband away in the Army, but this was the fate of thousands of women in wartime and many never saw their husbands again. But we all got on well together and settled down. I was sorry for my mother who was nearly sixty, after a lifetime with servants, but it was a question of just getting on with it. She and Babe shared the domestic chores and I became the gardener and handyman, both of which proved useful to me later. I soon learned to do electrical and other repair jobs, but gardening was more difficult. I sowed my first row of peas with each pea about a foot apart!

The first few months – the Phoney War – were uneventful apart from the war at sea, where German submarines were sinking a lot of our ships.

Then in June the French gave up completely and signed an armistice with the Germans. We were shocked. Britain was quite alone against the Germans and had to continue the war alone until the USA finally decided to help us eighteen months later.

It was no longer a Phoney War, but very real.

I Join the Land Army

THE great fear now was that the Germans were going to invade. They certainly intended to do so. All the coastal strip along the east and south coasts of the British Isles became a Defence Area. Our village of Ludham was within this, being only a few miles from the sea. The inland boundary was the river Ant and a disused windmill near Ludham bridge became a machine-gun post. All the beaches were mined and covered with obstacles and barbed wire. Very solid concrete 'pill-boxes' were built at strategic points such as crossroads; these were machine-gun posts and some were even disguised as kiosks selling ice-cream or as part of a school.

All cars left parked had to be put out of action, usually by removing the rotor arm and taking it away. Boats that were moored had to have all means of propulsion removed. All signposts were taken away, as were any indications of place names on shops or railway stations. This was supposed to confuse the invaders, so that they wouldn't be able to find their way! In fact, it confused travellers who got lost or arrived at a station to find the only signs they could see were 'Way Out' or 'Gentlemen'.

The Home Guard was formed as a local defence force and consisted of men too old, too young or too unfit to join the services, or men already doing essential work. In Ludham there was a very flourishing 'Dad's Army', as it became known, of about eighty men.

Summer 1940 was the time of the Battle of Britain. The German Air Force tried to bomb us into submission by destroying our airfields. That they didn't succeed was due to our marvellous Royal Air Force. These young fighter pilots, their beautiful and efficient Spitfires and Hurricanes, and the ground crews who looked after the planes combined to win a battle that was absolutely critical.

About this time Babe and I began to go out on our bikes on some evenings. There wasn't much entertainment; we were miles from the nearest cinema and there was no television in those days. We would go to an occasional dance, usually in Ludham Church Room, and we also went to some local pubs: the Kings Arms in Ludham and the Ferry Inn at Horning, a couple of miles away in the next village. This had a slightly more sophisticated clientele, including some of the fighter pilots from Coltishall, a local airfield. Here we made several friends, including a family who had moved to Horning to escape the daily bombing of Gt Yarmouth on the coast.

There was also a very nice young man of twenty, who was an agricultural pupil training on a farm at nearby Hoveton. Kingsley was tall with a nice face and dressed in tweeds and corduroys. We became firm friends and he lent me his classical records to play on my wind-up gramophone and gave me great bunches of daffodils. He told me that there were several Land Army girls working on the farm where he was. I realised that was what I should like to do, as I was happy working out of doors (my gardening having much improved), and I should soon have to do some sort of war work or join one of the services.

In April 1941 there was a Registration for Employment Order from the Government for all women between the ages of eighteen and forty-five years old. I was then eighteen, so I asked Kingsley if he could make enquiries about a job for me with the other girls at Hoveton Fruit Farm. He did this and it seemed that they were keen to have more girls.

So with a job in view, I went along to the Women's Land Army headquarters in Castle Street, Norwich, to see if I could 'join up'. In wartime one either joined up voluntarily or one was called up compulsorily. There I was welcomed by Iris Tillett, the Norfolk County Secretary, who was pleased to enrol me, especially as I had already acquired a job and could live at home, which meant that they didn't have to find either work or lodgings for me.

I was given my uniform: corduroy breeches, cotton dungarees, two aertex shirts, three pairs of long socks, a green jumper, shoes and a cowboy type hat. No rubber boots or outer garments. Wellies were in short supply and were reserved for dairy workers. I was lucky as my brother's rubber boots were available. They were a size too large, but I stuffed them with clean dry hay and kept warm and dry.

Later on I was sent an overcoat of brown cloth, but I never wore it for work. Also my pride and joy; a pair of old-fashioned black leather lace-up boots with nailed soles. These were terribly hard to start with, but later I wore them all the time, and a pair of canvas gaiters were supplied to go with them. We looked like farm workers of a previous century wearing them, but they were really rather snug. Apart from the shapeless breeches, it was quite an attractive uniform; the colours were pleasant, being green, fawn and brown. Also everything was made of wool, cotton or leather; no man-made fibres in those days. The breeches were laced just below the knee, the lacing being covered by the long socks, but they looked clumsy, even on slim and graceful girls – which I wasn't.

The Women's Land Army had existed during the previous war, having been set up in 1917 when reserves of food in Britain were very low. In those days it had been even more surprising to see women in breeches, although decently covered by long jackets, and doing agricultural work.

In 1938 Britain was importing 70 per cent of her food. By 1939 it was realised that there would be a shortfall of 50,000 farm workers, who were being called up to join the services. Ships bringing food were being sunk by submarines and there was an urgent need to get two million acres of land ploughed and growing crops by the following year. This was achieved, thanks in part to the girls, who were beginning to replace the men. The next year the quota was for a further million and a half acres to be cultivated.

By the end of 1942 all male farmhands over eighteen had been called up, which took a hundred thousand more men away from the land. In March 1942 alone, the submarines sank 275 of our merchant ships and by the start of 1943, imports of food to Britain were down to just half a million tons, the lowest since 1939.

The Land Army got to its maximum strength of 87,000 girls by July 1943. At that time, an agricultural journal, 'The Land Worker', which up till then had been sneering and scoffing at the idea of girls doing men's work, radically changed its tune and actually printed the following:

> *These women have to their credit magnificent records of successful efforts. They are doing the most valuable work and their organisation is essential to our war effort.*

Of course I had no idea of all this at the time, back in April 1941, when, duly clad in my new outfit, I climbed on to my bike for the half-hour ride to Hoveton Fruit Farm for my first day's work.

Starting Work

I FORGET now what time we started work, but I think it was 7.30 am in the winter and 7 o'clock in the summer. Anyway, I arrived in the main yard in front of the farm house where each day we waited in a shed for orders from the foreman, Herbert. As already described, the first day's work was in the carrot field, and that continued for a couple more days.

We were supposed to be given one month's training each. My training consisted of doing whatever job was down for that day and it soon settled into hoeing nearly every day. We hoed acres and acres of raspberry canes and strawberry plants and blackcurrant bushes, up and down the rows. I soon thought of a slogan: 'Join the Army and see the world, join the Land Army and hoe the bloody thing'. But it was pleasant enough work, though arms and backs ached terribly, and we chatted away all day long, working in pairs, one each side of a row.

The six land girls who were there when I arrived were all from nearby villages. Mary, Agnes and Joy were older than the rest of us and tended to form a group of their own. They did all the pruning. Doris was the daughter of the farm dairy man, then there was Hilda and another Doris, always known as Dimchie, as she was rather small. As ever, I was known as Pop, a nickname which I'd had since early childhood, and which has stuck all my life.

At the end of the first week I was very happy to receive my first wage packet from Herbert. At the start of the war the Land Army wages were 28 shillings for a forty-eight hour week (about £1.50 in today's money). Later the wage rose to 32 shillings, plus overtime. In 1944 it went up to 48 shillings. What riches! The girls who lived away from home had to pay for their board and lodging out of this, so I was well off, living at home, as were the other girls at Hoveton.

Saturday came and in the evening, Babe and I biked to the Horning Ferry Inn as usual. I had a long talk with Kingsley, all about the farm. I hadn't seen him all the week; it was a very large farm and he worked on the arable part, while I was on the fruit part. We saw our other friends, had a few drinks and biked home again at closing time. Little did we know that we should never see any of them again.

The second week's work was like the first, with lots of hoeing. My poor muscles were getting used to the exercise. The sixteen-mile bike ride was another form of exercise. Norfolk is reputed to be flat, but there seemed to be quite a few hills on my ride and always a head wind. Still, uphill one way meant downhill going back and there was a lovely flat bit across the marshes by Ludham bridge, with a view for miles, with several windmills visible.

I noticed lovely breakfast smells coming from some houses along the road in the early mornings. Evidently some people still had bacon! It made my mouth water, as I'd had a hurried breakfast of tea, toast and jam. My lunch would be sandwiches, made by me the previous evening, and it was difficult to find something to put into them. As manual workers, doing heavy work, we were entitled to eight ounces more cheese ration per week than other people, but it was mostly a rather dry Cheddar.

Ration books first appeared in January 1940 and the allowance per person per week was 4 ounces of bacon or ham, 4 ounces of butter and 12 ounces of sugar. Meat rationing began in March, by price, with one shilling and ten pence worth for an adult and eleven pence worth for a child under six. This was later reduced to even less. Offal wasn't rationed but hard to obtain. In July 1940, tea was rationed at 2 ounces per person, cooking fat was 2 ounces and butter was reduced to 2 ounces also.

A points scheme came in for tinned goods and other extras – when available – and everyone had sixteen points a month, later twenty, to spend on things like tinned salmon or fruit, condensed milk, biscuits, cereals or whatever they could find, as everything was scarce. Things like lemons and bananas completely vanished, and many children had never seen one. Oranges were reserved for pregnant women and small babies. Our chauffeur sent us a parcel of lemons from the Middle East and my brother sent us some dates from Iraq.

Eggs became scarce and dried powdered egg appeared. It was all right for cooking, but of course you couldn't produce a fried or boiled egg with it, only scrambled eggs or an omelette. The chaps in the services had most of the real eggs and it was traditional for aircrew to get two eggs before leaving for a raid. For too many, it was their last meal. Dried milk appeared with a small ration of liquid milk from November 1941.

In fact, rationing in Britain was very fair and adequate and we swapped and exchanged things between ourselves. It was said that the British people were never so healthy as during the war and this was true, but it was difficult for housewives to produce meals to satisfy everyone.

Saturday evening came round again. My mother decided that she would like to go out for a change, and have a drink and a chat. There wasn't much entertainment in her life in those days. She didn't ride a bike and the Kings Arms pub at Ludham was only about half a mile away. So Babe stayed home with little Margaret, and I walked down to the pub with my mother. As usual it was full of locals and people we knew and there was a piano in one bar, on which someone usually thumped out a tune and others would sing and it was a cheerful atmosphere.

Halfway through the evening I walked home and took over as the baby sitter, while Babe went to the pub and eventually walked home with my mother at closing time.

In those days, each village had its own policeman with a house for him to live in. Hillview was next door to the Ludham police house and we were friendly with the Sergeant and his wife and son.

Sometime during the Sunday morning, Arthur the son, who was my age, called me over to the dividing hedge. He was obviously upset. He told me the dreadful news that the Ferry Inn had received a direct hit on the bar from a lone German bomber. It had happened at 9.45 pm at the end of the evening, when the bar was full of people. Twenty-one were dead; all our friends, the elderly barman and six RAF men who happened to be there. There were only three survivors, who were all injured.

Poor Arthur had been part of the rescue team with the terrible job of getting out the bodies. It was a dreadfully sudden introduction to the horrors of war and the poor lad was absolutely shattered. It was ironic that the family who had moved to Horning to escape their home town bombing had four members killed and one injured.

It is possible that the Ferry was hit because a nearby boatyard was building fast motor torpedo boats, or perhaps it was that lights were showing, reflected in the river when people were leaving. It was 26 April 1941 and if my mother had not decided that she would like to go out that evening, it is sure that Babe and I would have been there instead of the Kings Arms, and that we had both missed almost certain death by a lucky chance. It was a very sobering thought.

Poor Kingsley. Such a nice chap. They buried him in nearby Hoveton churchyard. He had lived with his mother, whom I hadn't met, and I think that they had come to Hoveton from somewhere else for his training. I found myself left with a pile of his classical records and I didn't know what to do about them. I could hardly call on his poor mother, so recently bereaved. She would not want to meet a strange girl, claiming acquaintance with her son. In the end, I decided to keep the records and, indeed, I still have them, sixty years later, but no suitable machine on which to play them. They have given me a taste for classical music, as well as memories.

Hoveton Fruit Farm

I HAD been at the farm for a month or so when another girl arrived. This was Ann, who became my lifelong friend. She had been working in forestry, an important branch of the Land Army as wood was needed for pit props in coal mines and many other uses, to replace the timber that had previously been imported. A little older than me, she had been a photographer before the war. Ann had to live in lodgings as she had come from London, but her landlady was reasonable, so it wasn't too bad and she could even have a bath once a week. Some land girls had terrible lodgings, with not enough to eat or hardly any bedclothes and primitive conditions. Like me, Ann had a half-hour's bike ride to work, but from the opposite direction.

While at Hoveton, she became an absolute expert at laying hedges, and the neat thick hedges that one sees today were laid by Ann in the 1940s. Laying a hedge consists of cutting it with a billhook and 'laying-in' shoots which were half split from their main branch so that they continued to grow sideways where they were woven in. This makes a thick impenetrable hedge.

Ann was not used to the Norfolk dialect, and one day Herbert told her to go to a marsh 'down by that ole carr' to do something or other. Poor Ann spent a very long time looking for a derelict motor vehicle. She never did find it, as a 'carr' is a group of trees, usually alder, that have grown up on a marsh.

There is a lot of marshland on the farm, as the entire southern boundary is the river Bure. There are two stretches of open water, Hoveton Great Broad and Hudson Bay. I never did see the Broad, but I knew Hudson Bay, a lovely place with a cottage where one of the farm men, John, lived with his wife and small daughter. It is known as World's End, as it is very isolated.

The entire estate consisted of about 1,200 acres and the fruit fields were mostly in the centre. The rest was arable and marsh. The yard for the fruit farm was centred around a nice old farmhouse, with the farm offices, the big cold stores for the apples, sheds for tractors, workshops and tools. There was another yard for the arable side of the farm, where the dairy and the blacksmith's forge were. The forge was a lovely place to eat one's dinner on a cold day, but we didn't often have the luck to be anywhere near it.

The head of the arable farm was 'Squire' Ingate, who always rode his horse for work, being quite the best way to get from one side of the estate to the other and to approach men working in the fields.

The fruit farm manager was Mr Grainger, who lived with his wife in a house on the farm. They were very kind to me and once, when I was working overtime one evening, they brought me a lovely tray of tea, which I much appreciated as it was a long time since my dinner sandwiches and I had not expected to work overtime.

The owner of this estate, and my then employer, was Mr Thomas Blofeld. His obituary in the *Daily Telegraph* in 1986 wrote of him as 'The beau ideal of a country gentleman' and it is a perfect description. We didn't see much of him, but sometimes he would come across us doing some job, and he would stop and say a few words to us, usually ending with 'Well done, you!' in his aristocratic voice.

The Blofeld family home is Hoveton House, at the centre of the estate, nicely hidden by trees and gardens. Built by their ancestors in 1667, it is a beautiful house of red brick with Dutch gables. I hardly ever saw the house when I worked there, but much later, after the war, I was able to visit it with the Norfolk and Norwich Archaeological Society, which was a great privilege, as it is not open to the public.

The next girls to arrive on the farm were Gwen and Eileen, friends who came together. Gwen was a hairdresser who came from Norwich. Eileen had been a model and she looked the part. Tall, always neat and tidy, she could do really dirty jobs and still remain immaculate with her hair in a turban. We all envied her this ability. She and Gwen lived in lodgings on the farm itself.

The seasons went round and in the autumn we picked apples. For this, we each had a canvas bucket strapped on our shoulders. 'Treat 'em like eggs!" was the continual cry from Herbert, as apples are fragile and must not be bruised. The buckets opened at the bottom, to let the apples fall gently into a crate. It is easier to pick from the ground, of course, but trees had to be climbed and ladders used for the tree tops. There were lovely apples at Hoveton, all the old varieties that one never sees today. The cookers: Bramley, large, green and solid; and Derbys, even larger, but light for their size. The eating apples: Coxes Orange Pippins; Worcester Permain, an early apple that didn't keep long; Norfolk Royals, bright red; Russets, dull brown; and many others, whose names I forget, but all tasted so good. The rule on the farm was 'Eat all but pocket none', so we ate when we felt like it.

My first winter at the farm was a hard one. It was bitterly cold with snow in January and February and all the girls were put on to picking sprouts. The sprout plants were close together and we had to straddle each one, holding the leaves back with our legs, in order to pick the sprouts, put them into a small sack, and when we had filled two, carry them to the edge of the field where there was a weighing machine, weigh the sacks and tie them up. This was paid piece work, so much a sack. So it was up to us to fill as many as possible.

This was difficult: the plants were frozen stiff and covered in snow, the sprouts were full of bits of ice and we couldn't wear gloves, and our sleeves and trousers were soaked with melting snow. The farm soon provided us with fishermen's black oilskin trousers. These were waterproof but rather large and some of us, like little Dimchie, were rather small. Her trousers came up to her ears! We laughed hysterically, especially when we fell over. This happened a lot, carrying sacks amid the twisted stalks. The trouble was that, once we fell over, it was impossible to get up again without help in those stiff trousers and we lay there in the snow and ice, like upturned beetles, until hauled to our feet by a couple of chums. But there were compensations; I shall always remember the skeins of wild geese honking overhead in the dawn sky every morning. It was a beautiful sight. A pity we haven't any photographs, but films were scarce and there was no time; we were there to work.

Slightly better jobs included things like shuffling along on our knees planting cabbages or tiny onion plants the size of darning needles. Herbert would come along behind us and tweak the cabbages to see if we had planted them firmly enough and, if we hadn't, we had to go back and do them again. Thanks to this I have remembered all my life that brassicas need to be planted firmly and I still try to do so.

There was a large field of several acres of strawberry plants. In spring we filled the rows with straw between the plants and tucked it under the leaves, so that the fruit would not touch the earth and stay clean. In June we picked the strawberries with the gang of casual women, who were employed for all fruit picking. We worked on our knees and the straw made it comfortable. As it was warm, I had a tendency to fall asleep, especially if I had been out late the previous night. Ann used to turn round and prod my recumbent figure before Herbert saw me. After whole days of seeing strawberries, one had a red haze with pips when you shut your eyes.

We picked raspberries, we picked pears and we picked plums. Most of this fruit was sent away from the railway station at nearby Wroxham. Many apples went into the cold store on the farm. Here they had to be sorted and graded, and we stood beside a conveyor belt which brought them along and we wrapped them in thin paper and packed them neatly into trays. These then had to be stacked in the cold store. It wasn't terribly cold, just rather chilly. I think it had something to do with carbon dioxide, but nobody had time to explain things like that then. Once I trapped a nipple while stacking trays in the store. Of course I yelled; it hurt. I said it was my finger to avoid comments.

When the potatoes were harvested we were put to work in a field of about eight acres. A horse-drawn machine went up and down the rows. It had a revolving wheel with spoon-like attachments which neatly spun out the spuds. We each had a few yards to look after and had to get the potatoes all picked up and into sacks before the machine came round again. One had to get a move on. Once I picked up a potato and was surprised to find that it was hot. I looked more closely and discovered that my soil covered potato was in fact a piece of horse muck.

I Become Mechanised

ONE day Ann and I were together loading black-currant prunings onto a cart drawn by an elderly horse. It is very difficult to pick up twiggy prunings with a pitchfork and we already had a few giggles when what we hoped was a good forkful ended up as a couple of twigs. Most unusually two soldiers were sent to help us. Goodness knows where they came from. We were all a bit shy. The horse had a cough. In fact he coughed quite a lot. The trouble was, that every time he did so, he farted loudly. The soldiers were complete strangers to us so we tried hard to keep straight faces. It was impossible and all four of us collapsed into helpless laughter. I think the horse laughed too.

After I had been at the farm a while, I was asked if I should like to drive a tractor. I was very happy to do so as I have always liked machines. So I was introduced to the Allis Chalmers, a small tractor used for light field work and carting on the roads. This was going to change my type of work completely. For one thing, I should often be working on my own. This didn't bother me as I am quite happy by myself, although I should miss the talk and laughter with the other girls. We had now become eleven with the arrival of Pat from nearby Horning.

I was given no training, just a few explanations from 'Old' Bob, who wasn't old at all but terribly kind and much liked by all the girls. He was a wizard with motors and had a lovely sense of humour. A confirmed bachelor, he lived in a tiny cottage on the eastern edge of the farm.

Tractors at that time were rather different from those of today. There was no battery, so no lights or starter button, just a crank handle, usually fixed. The Allis was easy enough to crank, but she had a horrid tendency to kick. I soon learned to keep my thumb with my fingers round the handle and my legs out of the way, as I did not want a broken thumb or bruised shins.

Old Bob had a good laugh at me one day. The Allis had plugs that oiled up quite often and I was forever testing them with the motor running and a screwdriver and then cleaning the oily one when I found it. That day I was wearing large gloves and as I touched the plugs, the gauntlet touched the motor casing and sent a nice electric shock up my arm to my ear! Not realising what was happening, I yelped and jumped every time. Old Bob was doubled up with laughter.

There weren't any brakes on the Allis. There was a lever on the back wheels each side of the seat, presumably to turn sharply by hauling on one, but I

never found any use for them. You couldn't brake
with them; you'd have to take both hands off the
steering wheel and it would stall the engine. The rear
wheels and axle were very heavy compared with the
front ones, and this gave her a tendency to be back
heavy and to rear up if there was too much weight on
the drawbar or if the implement behind dug in too
deep. I didn't find out about this until it caused my
first accident. I was to have five accidents, but I survived. Tractor driving is quite a dangerous occupa-
tion, even on flat land. There were one or two quite
steep slopes around. One was just a small one in an
apple orchard.

I had been sent to the station to collect a load of
basic slag. This was a fertiliser made from the residue
from blast furnaces. I had two men with me, John and
Archie, and we unloaded it from the freight wagon in
the goods yard. We noticed that it was damp and
wobbly, rather like chocolate blancmange and the
same colour. The trailer was large and flat with low
sides and just two wheels in the centre. We set off
back to the farm with our rather unstable load and all
was well until we reached a slight downward slope in
the orchard. Luckily John and Archie had got off and
were walking beside me. The next thing I knew I was
upside down looking into the chocolate blancmange
which, being unstable, had run forward and the
weight on the draw-bar had tipped up and stalled

poor Allis. Her front wheels and engine were pointing to the sky. I climbed off carefully and now it was
me who was wobbly. So I sat down by a tree and we
looked in amazement at the upright tractor. Realising
that she was still in gear, I carefully leaned over her to
put her in neutral. We were all horrified when she
came back to earth with a terrific crash! Neither the
tractor nor I were any the worse for our adventure, so
we all carried on and spread the fertiliser around the
orchard.

I often went to the station either to load fruit into
the wagons or to collect something for the farm.
Another fertiliser was called shoddy. This had a sort of
woolly texture and came, I think, from textile factories. It was like the fluff that one finds in the bottom
of pockets. Everything was used that could possibly
serve and would not have to be imported. Once we
were sent to get a load of dried sewage. This was
white and flaky and not at all offensive. This caused
much mirth among my crew when they found – or
pretended to find – dried condoms! I got used to
climbing into freight wagons and once I managed to
cadge a short ride on a locomotive.

When there was a big load I always had a crew of
one or two men. They were all so very nice and good
humoured. John was my favourite; he was so calm
and kind, even though I involved him in two of my
accidents. Or there might be Archie, who lived

nearby, or Ernie, who lived on the farm, or Jack, who had a broad smile and a wooden leg, but could ride a bike as fast as anyone else. There were others on the fruit farm and quite a few on the arable side, but I saw less of them.

My second accident was my own fault. I was pulling a cultivator in an old orchard where the trees were large. Most had thick branches growing out low from the trunk. Fruit trees need to be kept low to make picking easier. I had a scarf tied round my head as usual, otherwise my hair got full of weevils and bits of twig. There was a mirror on the Allis for road work and I was looking at myself in this to adjust my scarf. I didn't see the huge branch looming up in front until it squashed me over the metal seat back and the engine stopped. Here was a problem; I was on my own, invisible amongst the trees and unable to move.

Luckily my guardian angel in blue overalls was working in another orchard not far away. Old Bob heard the sudden and prolonged silence and decided to investigate. I don't remember how he released me from my plight, but apart from a bit of skin scraped off my back and what felt like a flattened bosom, I was all right and carried on working.

Once I was bowling along the main road when the King and Queen overtook me. I didn't realise it at the time, but I did see a nice car with a flag on the bonnet, and I heard later that they had been on a visit in the area. In wartime there was hardly any traffic on the roads, apart from long army convoys or people doing essential work.

At some point the twelfth and last girl to join our gang arrived. This was Enid, who lived just beyond Ludham and had an even longer bike ride than I did. We often met and rode along together which was very pleasant. She was a very jolly person with a great sense of humour and we became firm friends. Enid would eventually take over the Allis Chalmers from me, but she began by doing general field work like the others. We worked together a lot later on, being the only tractor drivers among the girls. We both became good mechanics as we were supposed to look after the tractors ourselves and keep them in good order. I had begun to acquire quite a tool kit of my own.

There were five tractors on the farm and three men drivers, Sid, Arthur and Old Bob, who mostly drove the Bristol. This was a small machine with caterpillar tracks like a tank and a joystick instead of a steering wheel. It was narrow enough to be used between rows of blackcurrant bushes or raspberry canes. I used it sometimes and it was fun to drive. The first time I got onto it was on sandy soil and I pushed too hard on the stick and the Bristol spun round and round like a top.

I also drove the big three-wheeler Allis Chalmers a

couple of times, but the seat was perched up so high that it made me nervous. It straddled two rows of bushes, with its three wheels each in a different row.

One I liked very much was the big Fordson with a powerful Perkins diesel engine. The crank handle was long as it needed to be turned by two people. When I used this in the arable fields, I had to leave the engine running throughout my lunchtime, as there was no way that I could have started it on my own. So I used to start work again as soon as I had eaten my sandwiches, as it seemed such a waste of diesel to leave it running. On cold winter mornings the Perkins took ages to start, and I liked to watch two chaps thrusting a flaming rolled-up newspaper into its interior before they could crank the handle together. The fifth tractor was a petrol/paraffin Fordson which would become mine one day when Enid took over the Allis. This Fordson was solid and trouble free.

In the meantime I continued to work with Allis much as before and the war went on. Norwich, which was fifteen miles away, was bombed badly in 1942 and some nights we could hear the distant 'crump' of exploding bombs, and the German bombers flying overhead on their way there.

The Royal Air Force Arrive

As the war progressed our social life steadily improved. At the end of 1941 a small airfield was built in Ludham for fighter planes, and it was well placed, being near the east coast. The RAF moved in and began operations at once. They were flying Spitfires, probably the most beautiful and efficient fighter planes ever built. Babe and I began to meet several of the pilots in the pub or at dances.

I shall never forget those wartime dances. There was an atmosphere there that we shall probably never know again. We danced in any building that had a floor large enough: mess hut, church room or village hall. The music was provided by a gramophone, playing those lovely nostalgic 1940s records with a wartime theme: 'We'll Meet Again', 'Wish Me Luck As You Wave Me Goodbye', and 'There'll Always Be An England'. The young men came from all over the world: Canada, Norway, Australia, France, Poland, Czechoslovakia, Belgium, Holland, New Zealand and other places. They were all far from their homes and a bit lonely. Some had escaped from the Germans to come and fight with us for freedom. All were in uniform and many of the women too. Being in the Land Army, which was not a military service, we could wear our pretty dresses and high heels. One was never without a partner as there were always more men than girls. I remember dancing an old-fashioned waltz with a young pilot from Czechoslovakia. He was easy to follow and we whirled around the room at high speed. I didn't get giddy as he expertly changed direction all the time and I was wishing that I was wearing a crinoline.

Sometimes there was a Paul Jones, which was a dance which began with the girls in a ring, facing a ring of men, and we moved round to the music and when it stopped, the person opposite you was your partner, until the music changed again and you found another one. This was a good way of meeting people. The last dance of the evening was always a waltz, usually 'Goodnight Sweetheart', and it was all very romantic, in spite of the setting, and many hoped to really find romance. I was lucky. I did.

I met Scottie, who came from Southern Rhodesia (now the ill-fated Zimbabwe) and who was a Sergeant Pilot in 610 squadron. He was nice-looking with a large moustache, which was a trade mark of pilots in those days. Scottie was twenty-three and I was nineteen and we got along well from the start. We met again after the dance and he began calling to see us at Hillview. Then he acquired a bike from somewhere and would ride out in the evenings with us, when he was off-duty.

After the loss of the Ferry Inn we had started going to Sutton Staithe, a popular small hotel and country club about five miles away. Sometimes we would have a drink in the Sergeants' Mess with Scottie and the other chaps and got to know most of them. But one never knew whether the man to whom you were chatting in the evening would be there the next day, or whether he would be at the bottom of the sea or burned to death or just missing. Somehow one learned to accept this.

Scottie got the habit of flying low over Hillview and 'beating us up' when he came back from a sortie, to let us know that he was back safely. This made a terrific noise and made us all jump and the dog bark! I used to rush out and wave. He would also fly low over the farm and find me on my orange tractor and circle around me a few times. It used to be said on the farm that you always knew where Pop was working, as there would be a Spitfire overhead. I was biking to work one early morning, when Scottie found me going along the road across the marshes. This was an ideal place for low flying and he circled around me and my bike several times. The cockpit hood was open and his scarf blew out in the slipstream and was lost.

'Beat ups' were really a dangerous flying manoeuvre and were not encouraged by authority, although they mostly turned a blind eye to them. It was the same for 'victory rolls', which were a low roll over the airfield to show that a returning pilot had shot down an enemy plane. I had the great sadness to see from my attic window a victory roll which went wrong. The aerodrome was about a mile away and I saw an incoming Spitfire rolling, when, to my horror, it went down and a column of black smoke came up. It turned out to be a French pilot, whom I knew slightly.

Some time later another pilot thought that he would beat me up on the farm. The trouble was, I hardly knew him and he obviously had no idea where I worked, for he flew to Ludham Hall which was a Land Army hostel and found a girl on a tractor. She must have had an awful shock when he suddenly swooped down out of the sky! Pulling up, he caught the telephone wires along the road with his wing, dragged the wires over a nearby house, demolishing a chimney, then came down in a forced landing on the marshes.

The Spitfire was hardly damaged and the pilot escaped with a bruised nose. It took about three weeks to get that plane from its inaccessible position, the marshes being crossed only by narrow tracks and water-filled dykes. Each time I biked past I felt guilty, but it wasn't my fault at all, as I had not known anything about it till afterwards. In the war every plane was badly needed and the pilot got a severe reprimand for unauthorised low flying and disobedience of orders.

One of my most cherished memories of that time was of a foggy evening when I had biked to the airfield and was chatting to Scottie in the Mess, when suddenly B Flight was called to Readiness. This meant that they must go to the dispersal hut and await orders for take-off. It was dark and it was foggy. Crow, the flight commander, said that they would be unlikely to take-off in those weather conditions and that I could come with the chaps to the B Flight hut. So my bike and I were loaded into a lorry with the pilots and we set off across the airfield. This was totally against all military rules as I was a civilian and had no business to be there at all.

The flight hut was literally a wooden shed on the perimeter of the runways. Here, pilots sat around, dozed, played cards or read while waiting for the phone to ring. The aircraftman on duty would answer it and at once announce the message. If it was urgent, the order would be given to 'Scramble' and all would dash out to their planes, wearing fleece-lined flying jackets, warm flying boots and silk scarves with, on top of all this, their inflatable life jackets known as Mae Wests. It was cold in the sky and even colder if they got shot down into the sea. That evening the phone didn't ring at all while I was there; no Scramble and no Stand Down. The gramophone was playing and I remember Crow putting on a record of the Warsaw Concerto and asking me if I'd seen the film. It was the theme music from 'Dangerous Moonlight', a film about a Polish pilot, which I eventually saw, and that beautiful music will always remind me of that evening in the dispersal hut.

When it was getting late I thought I'd better go home, so Scottie helped me and my bike over a nearby hedge onto the lane to the village. As I pedalled home in the foggy night I realised that I had been very privileged indeed to be allowed to join the pilots on Readiness, and I imagine that few other civilians have ever done so.

Once I was sent by Hoveton Farm to do a few days' work at How Hill, a small fruit farm in Ludham, very near to my home. I took the Allis to Ludham with my bike and a small cultivator on a trailer. There was an orchard of large cherry trees at How Hill and it was very pleasant working beneath the cherry blossom. Even more so when I was joined by Scottie, the airfield being only a few fields away. He spent some hours with me each day, squashed with me on the tractor seat, much to the amusement of the foreman who had the appropriate name of Mr Bloom.

From there I was able to pop home to a proper meal at midday, instead of the eternal sandwiches. Also there wasn't the long bike ride morning and evening, so that I had more time at home. These facts made me think seriously that it might be a good thing if I could find a job nearer home.

Sometime during that summer Scottie was posted to Malta. Obviously at the time, I didn't know where he was going. All military movements were very secret. There were posters around and notices in newspapers with slogans like 'Careless Talk Costs Lives' or 'Be Like Dad, Keep Mum', which were illustrated by well-known cartoonists.

He went to Malta on the aircraft carrier Eagle in a big convoy that was badly bombed and torpedoed on the way. Malta was important to Britain because it was in a very strategic position in the Mediterranean which was vital for our defence of North Africa, where fierce battles were going on in the desert. It is a tiny island and it was attacked continually by the Italians and Germans. The death rate among our pilots was high and conditions there were difficult because ships trying to bring supplies were bombed and torpedoed all the time.

Great was my relief when he came back safely some months later, having walked the last miles from the station. As I opened the door to him, the radio was playing a tune called 'At Last, My Love Has Come To Me'. For supper my mother opened a treasured tin of Spam for him (a sort of spiced ham), only to discover that he had been living on the stuff all the time in Malta, and not much else.

Scottie had leave after being overseas. I asked for a week off work and we took the train to London where we had a happy time staying at the Regents Palace, just off Piccadilly. We wandered around and looked at the shops, but had no spare coupons for buying anything. We visited Rhodesia House and we frequented a pub called the Chandos Arms, where Rhodesians and other pilots gathered in the evenings. London was having a respite from bombing and there were no air raids while we were there. We went to the Zoo with another Rhodesian and his girlfriend and he and Scottie persuaded the keeper in the lion house that they missed seeing the lions so much, that he let us all in behind the cages where they were fed in much smaller cages, snarling over great lumps of meat. We were very close to them and it was quite frightening!

The Daily Round

WITH late nights and getting up early every morning, I was having difficulty staying awake on the tractor. On a warm sunny day with the noise and warmth of the engine, the never-ending effect of little apple trees going past me was like counting sheep. There was a very long orchard of young trees and it took ages to get from one end to the other. I tried everything to stay awake: singing, reciting poetry, spitting on my fingers and wetting my eyelids – all in vain. Somehow I managed to wake up enough to turn round at the ends of the field. Surprisingly I only once got into difficulty, when the small set of disc-harrows got caught around a tree. This was a problem, as discs could not be reversed and were too heavy to un-hitch and move manually. Somehow I found a lever and heaved the dead weight over without damaging the tree. Off I went up the row again, my head soon starting to nod.

One spring Enid and I were given the job of applying a pesticide powder to apple trees. We had to start work at 5 am when there was no wind. We towed the dusting machine into position, having filled it up with powder. Starting it was a real problem and terribly dangerous. It had a large flywheel and the crank handle was in the centre of this, a long handle, as it needed two people to turn it. As soon as we got it going, with a roar like an air-raid siren, the heavy handle would fly off with tremendous force. The first time we did it, we looked at each other in horror, and ever after, when we cranked, we would throw ourselves flat on the ground away from its trajectory, but we never knew where it would go! It was absolutely lethal and could easily have killed somebody. There was also another danger that no one gave a thought to in those days: how toxic was the pesticide? We worked in clouds of white powder and must have breathed some in. Anyway, we have both survived into old age.

Sometimes in the summer when it was very hot, some of us would go down to the river during our lunch break and have a swim, usually in our underwear. There were no boats on the rivers in those days, apart from the odd army patrol boat. I don't think that anyone ever saw us, an assorted collection of pink nymphs enjoying the cool water.

Winter was a different matter. We worked in all kinds of weather. If it was really bad we were given an inside job, but there wasn't really much that could be done under cover, apart from in the apple store and that was usually all finished before the mid-winter.

Opening up potato clamps was a cold job for winter. The clamps were large and covered with straw and earth. When opened up, the few potatoes that had gone bad stank to high heaven. We would have a little bonfire going nearby to try and give some warmth, as we didn't move much. We sorted the spuds, good ones into sacks and the squishy smelly ones on to a heap. Gloves got soaked and filthy and weren't much use. In bad weather we wore jute sacks as they are almost rain-proof, if a bit prickly, and they smelt lovely and earthy. I cut holes for my head and arms and wore mine as a tunic, belted with a bit of string. We became very adept at finding sheltered spots under a hedge in order to eat our lunches in the rain or snow. If we were anywhere near the black-smith's forge, that was lovely and warm, and often became quite crowded.

When the roads were icy it was difficult biking to work and we often fell off, especially on black ice. My irreplaceable thermos flask was soon broken, and glass bottles of cold tea went the same way. Plastic bottles had not yet been invented. One day when the snow was really deep, I set out to walk to work. There was no traffic, just a coal lorry, struggling through the drifts, which gave me a lift.

One Christmas Ann and I did a naughty thing. Near Hoveton House there was an old orchard with lots of mistletoe on the apple trees. It was dark when we finished work, so we hid our bikes and crawled into the orchard on our hands and knees. A dog barked and gave us a fright, but no one saw us and we took a small bunch of mistletoe each, which certainly improved our Christmas spirit and I'm sure was never missed.

Scottie had left his trunk at Hillview, rather than take it around with him every time he moved. There was a bag of tobacco from Rhodesia in it, which he had told me to give away. I thought of Old Bob, who always rolled his own fags. I had previously given him a little of our tea ration when my mother could spare it, as one person living alone didn't fare very well on two ounces a week. So, one day, in a bit of a hurry, I gave him a bag of tobacco and dashed off. How we laughed later when he told me that he had made tea with it! It was a better smoke than a drink.

One day I was bowling along on the Allis to a village a few miles away where some fields were used by Hoveton Farm, mostly for potatoes. I had an empty trailer and John and Archie were sitting on it. We had to cross a single track railway over an open crossing with no gates. Maybe I went up the slope too slowly, for Allis stalled her engine in the middle of the railway line. An ancient steam locomotive was chugging towards us at full speed. Luckily they were looking where they were going and stopped beside us, with a few ribald comments. I restarted the motor and off we went again.

A spectacular accident with the Allis happened on a pouring wet day. Quite late in the afternoon Herbert told me to take two trailers and fetch as much steam coal as possible from the station, as it was needed for threshing the next day.

Two trailers were a lot for the little Allis, as they held about one and a half tons each. Once again, John and Archie were with me and we all wore sacks over our shoulders to try and keep the rain off. We unloaded the coal from a wagon, using shovels for the small stuff and our hands for the big lumps. We were wet and we were black. We loaded both trailers well and there must have been nearly two tons on each. We had to deliver the coal at North Farm on the Hoveton estate, where there was quite a steep hill down to the farm, with a dyke, crossed by a narrow bridge at the bottom.

All that coal was too much for poor Allis's engine. We gathered speed rapidly going downhill with the load pushing the tractor. There was nothing that I could do to slow her down, as there were no brakes. Somehow I managed to steer a straight course and get us over that narrow bridge where we skidded out of control on the other side, and came to a sudden stop, facing in the opposite direction with the front wheels just on the water's edge. I looked round. Coal every-where. Not a sign of my crew. Then two black faces slowly appeared out of the long wet grass where they had jumped off as we skidded. We had to laugh, mostly with relief. Then we had to turn the trailers round, extricate the tractor and pick up all the scattered coal, then finally deliver our load into a barn a bit farther on.

We went home late, weary, very black and sodden wet.

Ludham Village at War

LUDHAM, like other villages in the British Isles, remained outwardly unchanged during the war, in spite of unusual things which happened there during those years. There was no population census taken in 1941 and the number of the inhabitants was estimated at about 875 people. It would have been difficult to count, as many of the usual inhabitants were away on active service or other work, while at the same time there were hundreds of men on the airfield and in the small army camp who were not usually there.

The first soldiers had arrived with a searchlight in 1940. There were only about a dozen of them, so they were often invited to people's homes for cups of tea and hospitality. When they came to Hillview for a cuppa, they usually repaid us by pumping up water with the hand pump in the garden. It was a change from army duties. The searchlight moved away after about a year, but after the war one of the lads returned to marry a local girl.

During the war various campaigns were organised to raise money for different causes, the aim being to buy an aeroplane or a tank, and there was great rivalry between towns and villages to raise the most money.

We had 'Wings For Victory' week and 'Salute the Soldier' week and many others. There was usually a parade of military and civil defence to open such a week, and I remember one in Ludham in the wide main street, where a well-known General took the salute. There were large companies of Army and Royal Air Force, Air Raid Wardens, Home Guard, a few nurses and even a contingent of the Women's Land Army. There were quite a lot of us; the hostel at Ludham Hall numbered about thirty, as well as land girls from farms all around. Our local Land Army representative had said that I was to lead this group. I don't know why I was chosen, perhaps it was because I lived in Ludham. Anyway, we all turned out looking smart and tidy, wearing our hats and armbands with our green jumpers and breeches. We marched along behind the forces and as we passed the saluting base, I could not resist giving a salute and an eyes-right. It seemed to be appreciated.

Since the start of the war there was a black-out all over the country, but as Ludham had never had any street lighting it didn't make much difference. Everyone had thick dark curtains over their windows or screens to fit. Air raid wardens looked for chinks of light showing and banged on the doors and shouted 'Put that light out!' Torches and batteries became very scarce. The few cars had black covers over their headlamps with just a couple of slits for light. My bike had a dynamo on the back wheel to work the lights, but when I slowed down, so did the lights. From February 1940 Summer Time was extended to last all the year, then in 1941 and 1942 we had Double Summer Time until the end of the war. It kept light till quite late at night.

Clothes and textiles were rationed from June 1941. Everyone got sixty-six coupons which were valued according to how much labour and material was needed for a garment. Women who could sew had an advantage (I couldn't) as they could make dresses and things out of old curtains or bedspreads. 'Make Do and Mend' became yet another slogan. We land girls were supposed to mend our clothes and darn our socks, but I used to just turn my socks around when there was a hole in the heel, until eventually the foot fell off. To save fuel, one could only have five inches of water in a bath. Soap was rationed from February 1942 and my mother used to boil up ends of soap to make a multi-coloured new piece.

The most tragic incident in Ludham happened on a quiet Sunday. It was the middle of the day and most families were sitting down to their Sunday lunch – such as it was in those days. One family were around the table in the flat over their grocer's shop in the centre of the village. A solitary German aircraft flew over low, spraying machine gun bullets at the houses. No doubt he was just amusing himself. One of his bullets hit the mother of this family and killed her as she sat at table. All the village were terribly shocked and sad, and it made one realise just how vulnerable we all were.

Another time a stick of bombs was dropped across the outskirts of the village, killing two horses in a stable just down the road from Hillview. We were worried as my father, who had retired and come to live with us by then, had walked down to the Kings Arms for an evening drink. Luckily he hadn't set off to return home when it happened. It was getting dark and the last bomb landed in the field behind Hillview. It was an incendiary and blazed furiously with a bright light. I set out in my slippers with a pail of water to douse it, when the policeman next door shouted to me to leave it alone, as it could explode. I turned back, very relieved.

In December 1943 an American plane – a Lightning with the name 'Vivacious Vera' painted on it – had engine trouble returning from a raid on Kiel. The pilot, flying on one engine and with other problems as well, made for the nearest airfield, which was Ludham. He was coming in over the village when the other engine stopped. He went through the branches of a large tree and crashed in a small yard behind Thrower's shop and the butcher's, where it demolished a stable, pigsty and shed, all empty. One engine went through the back of Thrower's garage with such force that it pushed a van out through the closed front doors!

Cyril Thrower, in his shop, heard all this and thinking that it was an air raid, sent his staff into the cellar. The tail of the plane crashed through the roof of his house, one wheel rolled several hundred yards right down the street and another large piece went through the garage roof. Across the street, Russell Brookes, working in his garage, dashed out and saw flames coming from the crashed plane. He and Cyril tried to pull out the pilot, but he was wedged by one foot trapped in the wreckage. Russell cut metal with boltcutters, but to no avail. The pilot was begging them to cut his foot off, so someone fetched a meat cleaver and a saw from the butcher's. The fire was increasing and ammunition was exploding and some more people were pulling hard when suddenly the pilot's foot came out of its boot and he was pulled free.

Meanwhile flames had reached Cyril's house and were licking the bedroom curtains, where his wife was nursing their baby son. The pilot was carried clear and everyone helped to extinguish the fire, including the local fire engine, which had just arrived on the scene.

Finally no great damage was done and the pilot had only minor injuries and shock, thanks to the bravery and coolness of Cyril Thrower and Russell Brookes and the other village people. Apart from occasional excitements like this, life was pretty quiet, but on many nights we would hear the drone of hundreds of enemy bombers flying overhead on their way to bomb the bigger towns and cities inland. Over 60,000 civilians were killed in Britain in this war and 237,000 injured.

Learning to Plough

AT Hoveton, Enid had begun to drive the Allis Chalmers and I was promoted to the Fordson, which I much preferred, as it was larger, heavier and stronger. One got on to it from the back and sat on a round metal seat on a spring, or it could be driven standing up on the footplates. I suppose that by now, I had become quite a good tractor driver. Reversing trailers was second nature to me, and it was a matter of great pride to me that I could reverse a trailer piled high with straw bales or crates into a barn door that I could not see.

One day I was told that I was going to learn to plough and that I was to go to one of the arable fields where Arthur would teach me. He drove the big diesel Fordson and was a nice calm chap who worked on the arable side of the farm.

First I learnt to set out the top. This was some way into the field, as you work round it afterwards in a rig. It was very difficult to head for a small white stick at the other side of the field in a dead straight line, to open the first furrow. Having arrived there, you turn on the headland and plough back, turning the soil right up against the first furrow, still keeping absolutely straight. This makes a slight ridge, which is the top, and you go on round and round this until you have a fair-sized piece of ploughed land, which is the first rig. Then you start all over again, with a top at the correct distance away, and plough another rig round that, until the two join up in a neat *straight* pair of adjoining furrows, which make a slight hollow. And so on, until the field is all ploughed and then you plough round the headlands.

Alas, no field in Norfolk is an absolute rectangle or square; they are all shapes, some ending in a point. All these odd-shaped corners are known as scoots or the scooty bits and they have to be ploughed in ever-diminishing furrows. After ploughing, the field is harrowed in the other direction, which flattens the tops and fills the furrow hollows and leaves a nice flat surface for drilling. If there are lumps and clods, it will have to be rolled as well.

After this, I often worked in the arable fields, as well as carting fruit and other jobs. Once I was working in a field when I heard a shrieking noise. To my horror, it was a rabbit, caught in a trap on the bank. One of those awful old traps with metal jaws, and this poor rabbit had one back leg caught in it. I dashed over and levered it open with a screwdriver and saw that the leg was just a dry bone. The poor creature must have been in there for a long time. Amazingly, it rushed off as soon as it was free.

Not long after this there was to be a pheasant shoot on the farm and we were told that we would be needed as beaters. Since the rabbit incident, I had become very anti-gamekeeper, so I said indignantly that I was there to work to help the war effort and not to act as beater for the guns. Herbert tried to persuade me by saying that I should miss the free beer! But while the rest of the farm enjoyed the shoot, I worked on my own, for the sake of one poor rabbit.

My last mishap with the Allis happened when Enid was driving it one day. We were going along the road with an empty trailer and I was balancing on the drawbar, talking to her. Enid turned round to see why I hadn't answered her last remark and was amazed to see me lying flat on the road some distance behind! I had fallen off the drawbar and gone under the trailer with the wheels each side of me. I wasn't hurt and we had a good laugh.

There was only one accident with the Fordson and it was not my fault. I was going along the road early one very frosty morning with no trailer behind and driving towards a brilliant sunrise. The frost and the sun together were absolutely dazzling and a man in a small car coming up behind just did not see the tractor and drove right into me. Luckily my legs were out of the way when he hit me, but it was a nasty surprise and did his little car no good at all.

There was an excellent carpenter in Neatishead, a

village several miles off the Hoveton to Ludham road. My mother had ordered a wheelbarrow from this man and it was ready to collect. There were no lorries or transport available to carry it home for us and the only solution was for me to push it home, a journey of about six or seven miles. So one evening after work, Enid and I biked to Neatishead and I took delivery of a heavy wooden barrow with an iron-shod wheel. Enid could ride a bike while pushing another one, so she set off homewards pushing mine and I set off pushing the barrow. It wasn't too bad as there was no traffic and it was a fine evening, but at some point, the wheel began to squeak. As I went on the squeak became louder and louder until it became a sort of howl. People began to come out to see what was going past. I was very embarrassed, but there weren't many houses along the road and I eventually arrived home with my noisy barrow. After a drop of oil it served us well for many years afterwards.

In 1942 we were very excited to learn that my father had been awarded an MBE and that he was commanded to go to Buckingham Palace to receive it. My mother didn't want to make the journey to London, so it was decided that I should accompany him. He was still living in my brother's house, so we had to go to our own home to find his morning suit and top hat. The suit was in the wardrobe, but the only hats we found were in the attic. One was an opera hat, in its original box, and the other was a Dickensian tall topper with a curly brim that must have dated from my father's young days in the 1800s. I said firmly that I would not go to the Palace with him in either of those, and then we had the good idea of using my brother's top hat, which fitted perfectly.

I set and pinned up my hair before going to bed, but I was so excited that I dreamed that I was getting ready and took all the curlers out in my sleep.

We arrived at the Palace in good time and I sat on a gilt chair and listened to the music. King George VI came in and the investiture began with a Victoria Cross for a naval officer. It was very impressive and beautifully done. When the name Thomas Robinson was called, I was surprised to see another man come in instead of my father. However, all was well: there were two Thomas Robinsons who were both awarded an MBE.

Shortly after this my father retired and came to live with us at Hillview. Much later, Babe and her small daughter went back to London to live. Air raids there were now much less frequent, and many people returned. She could live in her own house there now and be near to her parents and sisters. So our family changed around again and I missed my biking and drinking companion.

My twenty-first birthday came along almost unnoticed and I celebrated it with a few drinks with Scottie at the Hoveton Black Horse, a small pub on the farm estate.

One day I heard that there was a tractor driver's job available on a farm in Ludham, so I went along to apply for it and got the job. I gave in my notice at Hoveton Farm rather sadly.

Hall Common Farm

As I had imagined, there were many advantages in working near home. It was about five minutes' ride to the farm, two stretches of road and a short cut along a green lane. I had no more sandwiches to make and my cheese ration could be used for other things. Previously my mother had tried to save a part of the family lunch to heat up for me in the evenings, but this was not easy, as there often wasn't a lot of lunch in the first place. Another great help to our rations was that I could buy fresh milk from the farm, so every day a quart white milk churn dangled from my handlebars. We could have things like bread and butter pudding again, which had been horrid when made with dried milk. It occurs to me now that it was probably illegal to buy the milk, but no great quantities were involved as there were only five employees on the farm, including me, who bought it.

My new employer and his wife, Mr and Mrs Bert Richies, were a pleasant and kindly couple with a daughter, Brenda, then about twelve years old. Like Hoveton, their farmhouse was seventeenth century with the curved Dutch gables that are only found in East Anglia. The house was on a very much

Clockwise from top left: The author trying to knit for the troops in 1939; Hillview in 1940; Babe and Margaret with soldiers pumping water for us, 1940; Badges awarded to the author

The author showing off her new uniform

Above: The author on the Allis Chalmers 1942

Right: Picking apples – L-R the author, Dimchie, Joy and Pat *(Eastern Daily Press)*

Land girls at Hoveton 1941 Lunch time L-R, Pat, the author, Ann, Agnes, Mary, Dimchie, Doris and Hilda *(Eastern Daily Press)*

Picking apples at Hoveton 1941 L-R Doris, Hilda, Dimchie, Mary, the author (in tree) and Ann *(Eastern Daily Press)*

Making silage 1941; the author,
Agnes and some of the men

Joy on the load and the author on the
tractor, but only for the photograph

Raking silage 1941; L-R Ann,
Agnes and the author

John on the horse rake and
Herbert the foreman

Clockwise from top left:
The author, Scottie and Babe,
1942; Scottie and the author
1943; Scottie 1942; Scottie
and friend in my boat 1943

The Horning Ferry before the war (Old Postcard)

BOMBED: The wrecked Ferry Inn at Horning after it was hit by a German bomb killing 21 people 60 years ago.

The Horning Ferry after the bombing, April 1941 *(Great Yarmouth Mercury)*

Above: With other land girls.
Second and third from left,
author, Ann. Back row from
right, Mary, Agnes, Joy. Front
row from right, Hilda, Dimchie

Centre: The author on the
Fordson carting apples

Below: The author pulling up
blackcurrant bushes with
Ann on the Allis

A painting of Hall Common Farm by Colin Burns

The author on the
iron-wheeled Fordson

A Land Girl saluting a pilot.
A watercolour by Joan Snelling

smaller scale and had a thatched roof.

The whole farm was very much smaller; there were about eighty acres of arable fields and thirty of marsh and reed beds. It was situated on the edge of the upland and overlooked miles and miles of marshland. The coast was about five miles to the east.

The farmyard was large with many buildings. A small herd of cows occupied a straw-filled yard, partly roofed, with the milking parlour alongside. In fine weather they went down to the marshes to graze.

Mr Richies had hoped that I might learn to milk, so that I could relieve him on the cowman's day off. I tried hard, but I wasn't much good at it. A patient red-poll cow (no horns) stood quietly while I dug my head into her flank and fumbled about underneath. I saw that she had turned her head and was looking at me quizzically. I made my apologies to her, but it made no difference, barely a trickle of milk came. So the boss continued to milk once a week and I got the nice job of accompanying the small herd along grassy lanes to the marsh. I was happy, biking slowly behind them and looking at the wild flowers on the banks. One day I became aware of someone behind me and turned round to find a neighbour's bull trotting along just behind me. I left my charges and shot back to the farm in a panic. Mr Richies just laughed and said to bring the bull back with the herd and that it was not me that he was interested in.

Some large sows in the farmyard produced piglets from time to time and I often had to feed them. I would stagger into their pen with a heavy pail of pig swill in either hand and about fourteen small pigs would charge into my legs and the pails and once knocked me over. What a mess. Pig swill and pig muck, pigs, pails and me all mixed up. I also had to muck them out sometimes which was rather an aromatic job, but I really think that chicken muck smells much worse and I had to do those too.

There were some geese loose around the farmyard and I was scared of the gander. He knew this and would charge me with neck outstretched and wings flapping. Once we met at a corner of the house and I seized the nearest object, which was a dustbin lid, and used it as a shield, Britannia-like as far as Mrs Richies' kitchen door where I sought refuge. That aggressive bird was eventually run over by a car and killed. He attacked anything that moved.

There were four men employed on the farm, all getting on a bit. Jimmy was the eldest. Small and white-haired, he wore his trilby hat tied around under his chin with a piece of string in windy weather. Then there was Billy, red-faced and jolly; I already knew him, for these were all Ludham men. Roger the cowman was a bit younger than the others and had a marvellous flow of bad language. Jolt, the team man, was in charge of the horses and also a sort of foreman.

I never did know his correct name. He had a very broad Norfolk accent and I often had trouble understanding what he said. He was a man of few words and hated having to repeat things. I was to work with him a lot. Unlike the men at Hoveton, these were not at all used to having a girl – and a Londoner at that – to do the same work as they did.

The tractor was a good old Fordson, which had metal wheels with large studs in them, instead of tyres. This meant that it could not be driven on a road without first putting large flat metal bands around the back wheels to cover the studs. To avoid having to do this every evening, the tractor would be left in the field for the night, and covered with a tarpaulin.

The Land Army had started to have proficiency tests for the girls, in all the different branches of farming. I was entered for a tractor driver's test and duly transported in a bus with lots of other girls to West Barsham Hall. There we had both an oral and a practical test. There were questions about the maintenance of tractors and the uses of various implements. I was told to get onto a Fordson tractor with a two-furrow plough attached, and to lay out a top. Luckily I'd had quite a bit of practice by now, so I managed a fairly straight one. In all, I did well, getting over 90 per cent marks. I was told that I had lost marks by not being able to thread a binder. I had never done it, and it wasn't something that you could guess at. We all went home in the bus, happily clutching our new proficiency badges, which were made of bakelite, an early type of plastic.

Some time after this, the girls at the Ludham Hall Hostel invited me to go with them to a dance at an American base. This was a long way away and a lorry was sent to pick us up. It seemed that they needed some 'nice' girls to counteract the effect of the many perhaps not so nice girls who chased after the Yanks! Anyway, our lorry got lost in the dark twisting Norfolk lanes, and by the time we arrived very late at the dance, the second category of girls had taken over and we were left as wallflowers. I don't think that many of us had even one dance, but we tucked into the good food supplied and slept in the lorry on the long ride back.

Field Work

IT was lovely ploughing the big fields at Hall Common. Two of them were twelve acres and most of the others were seven or eight acres. They all had a lovely view: miles of marshland under a huge Norfolk sky, with clouds, birds and aircraft for extra interest. My furrows were always full of birds too, mostly sea-gulls, white against the brown soil, quarrelling noisily over the insects and often a wagtail or two, with their cheerful little faces, balancing on a furrow.

In a nearby field Jolt would be ploughing with two horses. Needless to say, his furrows were arrow-straight, after all, he had been doing it all his life. Mine weren't too bad, though I would often be surprised to find un-ploughed bits between my last furrows where the rigs joined. I had to go over these bits again to turn them over and that made it messy, although of course that did not really matter, as once the harrow had been over, all would be neat again, with nothing showing of my inexperience. The men would laugh and tell me not to mind, as the crops would grow just the same, and there were oft-repeated jokes about crows breaking their legs in my furrow.

I didn't like my work to be messy and if a field had

uneven scooty bits, I liked to start on these, as it made it much neater afterwards. I was doing just this one day in an odd little corner when the Guv'nor came along. He was a dear kind man, but a bit impatient and liked to get on with things, so he told me off rather sharply for not doing the main field first. In fact, it made no difference. He was horrified when his tractor driver burst into tears and rushed off back to the farm to tell his wife that he had upset me! It was silly of me and I must have been having an 'off' day, but I was upset to be told off when I was working hard.

Because of the wartime need to get all possible land producing food, many odd small bits were ploughed that normally would not have been. Long Pightle was one of these; barely two acres in extent, it was right on the edge of the marshes that stretched away to the river Bure and the ruins of St Benet's Abbey. I don't think it had ever been ploughed before. It was so long and narrow that it could not be worked crossways and it was thick with rushes and sedge. I seemed to spend a long time turning over this rough land and going over it again and again with a cultivator to break up the clods. It was at last sown with wheat by Jolt, but the crop that eventually came up could not have done much towards winning the war.

The tractor was left out in the fields at night, because of the metal wheel studs. In the winter I had to drain the radiator before covering it up with a large tarpaulin. Once I had been working all day in the rain and tractors in those days did not have cabs. It wasn't cold at the end of the day and being in a hurry to get home and dry I forgot to drain the radiator.

Oh dear. There was a terribly sharp frost that night and when I removed the tarpaulin the next morning, I was horrified to see great cracks in the cylinder block with ice protruding from them. The Guv'nor was just as horrified and paced up and down muttering. He was really awfully good about it and didn't blame me at all. I was terribly ashamed as I knew the problems of getting spare parts in wartime. In fact we seemed to obtain a new cylinder block very rapidly and work was able to continue.

On two occasions we had gangs of prisoners to harvest the potato crop. The first lot were Italian prisoners of war. I was the only female there of course, and I was glad to be isolated on the tractor. They worked well and gave me the pleasure of many dark handsome smiles!

The second lot were civilian prisoners from Norwich gaol. They were a pale-faced sad-looking lot and their warder was the only one that looked a real thug. Once again I was on the tractor all the time and wondering to myself just what crimes they had committed.

There was a lot of work apart from the tractor. I

spent days muck-spreading with a fork from muck-heaps previously placed there by Jolt from a cart. That did make my shoulders and arms ache; there were eight acres to be spread by just three of us. Being a winter job, it did keep us nice and warm.

Much colder were jobs like lifting mangel-wurzels, chopping them with a reaphook and throwing them into the tumbril. These were big golden outsize roots which were used for cattle feed, like swedes, which were also golden. No one had any idea at that time just how much agriculture would change after the war. But I did realise that the work we did and the tools and implements and methods that we used were practically unchanged since medieval times. Names like tumbril and 'morphra' for carts, mangel-wurzel, coombe, a measure of wheat, and many others were unchanged since then. 'Morphra' was an unusual one, being short for hermaphrodite, a cart that with a slight change had two uses. When I learned to 'broadcast' I realised that it was a really ancient practice, except that instead of sowing corn, we were scattering artificial fertiliser. A sack carefully tied around one shoulder made a bag to contain it, and we used the right hand to scatter evenly from left to right, moving forwards at a steady pace all the time. A truly biblical gesture.

Fields of sugar beet were hoed by the men on piece work. They were paid a sum for singling (thinning out) and removing weeds from a certain area. I was given the odd bits to do at my usual pay. I was much amused at what I used to call 'half hour conversations'. The men worked their given pieces, scattered far apart across the field. In the course of their work, two would pass near each other and would exchange a word or two. No time for lengthy talk on piece work. Onwards they went on hoeing. About half an hour later they would pass again and an answer or a further comment would be made and so on at intervals. They certainly had time for reflection.

One day some soldiers were practising firing something at a target on the marsh at the end of the field where I was working on the tractor. Not guns, some other weapon that made a lot of smoke, so I suppose they couldn't see me. I was working longways and had to pass fairly near at the end of the row, and I began to wonder if they might miss the target and hit me. Having no tin hat, I tried to balance a milk churn lid on my head, but, being heavy, it tipped forward and cut my nose, so I gave up the idea. I don't suppose that I was in any danger at all, unlike the land girls near the coast in Kent, who were under machine gun fire and bombardment most of the time. One girl was killed and the others grew expert at diving under their tractors or into a hedge. They were really brave girls.

The Horses

THERE were three horses at Hall Common Farm. Judy and Blossom, the two big Suffolk Punch mares, did all the heavy work. Tinker, an elderly black pony of about thirty years old, did odd jobs. He had spent his life pulling the paraffin cart around the village and was then retired to a comfortable life on the farm. He and I worked together quite often, although I wasn't used to handling horses and he knew this and took advantage of me whenever he could.

The morning when I went to fetch him from the marsh for the first time, I walked confidently across the grass, holding his bridle. He went off like a race-horse and the other two joined him and they galloped round and round me like a circus round the ring-master. I could see Jolt watching from the upland and roaring with laughter. He came to my rescue, took the bridle and just put it on to a now stationary Tinker. I was never again sent to fetch him and on the days that he was needed Jolt would bring him up with the mares and I collected him from the stable.

There again he managed to outwit me. I had to put all his harness on, ready for work, starting with his collar. Horse collars are very heavy and Tinker was taller than me, so I climbed on to the manger in order to push it over his head, having first undone the rope by which he was attached. That cunning animal turned round, went out of the door and was off back to the marshes as fast as his old legs would carry him. I was left standing in the manger, clasping the collar. I biked after him, brought him back and began all over again, having shut the door this time.

When he and I were put on to raking hay on a warm summer's day, he would fall asleep, going along more and more slowly while I dozed, sitting on the rake behind him. The Guv'nor had to shout at us occasionally to wake us up. Sometimes we used to cart things with the tumbril. Being the smallest and the lightest cart, it was suitable for him. After the sugar beet harvest was over, we would cart the green tops from where they were left in rows in the fields. The cows loved them. They also ate the residue that came back from the sugar factory as pulp. This was very sweet and I used to chew a bit myself sometimes. The entire supply of sugar in Britain came from home-produced beet at that time and no cane sugar was imported at all.

One day Tinker and I took a tumbril full of potatoes to somewhere beyond the village. I sat on the front of the cart and we ambled along at our usual gentle pace on the empty main road. Suddenly, from the opposite direction came a large squad of soldiers, running along knees up 'at the double'. Of course they were very pleased to see a land girl and they laughed and shouted while still thundering along the road. Poor Tinker was absolutely terrified at the noise and movement and stood upright between the shafts, tipping me and the cart back. I yelled at them to shut up and waved my arms about, but to no avail. They passed by and eventually left us in a blessed silence. I consoled a trembling Tinker, climbed back on to the cart and we went on again, both of us feeling a bit wobbly. I seemed destined to drive things that tipped me backwards; it was just like the Allis tractor used to do.

Another day we delivered sacks of spuds to a shop in the village. I carried the sacks of fifty kilos across my shoulders from the cart to the shop, bent under the weight. In fact it's not difficult, provided you are fairly strong and the sacks are at the right height. A passing soldier peered under the sack to see who was carrying it. He turned to his chum. 'It's a girl!' he said in amazement.

In the spring Jolt and I spent weeks horse-hoeing the sugar beet fields with one of the mares. Up and down the rows we went, me leading the mare and Jolt guiding the hoe. A horse is lovely and warm to work with on a cold day and I was close to her head, keeping her straight in one row. Once or twice she trod on my foot and sometimes her dribble blew across my face, but she was such a big, gentle creature that one could forgive her anything. The Suffolks are the oldest race of the big horses. They are a golden red colour and, unlike the Shire horses, have no long hair or 'feathers' on their feet.

We could not talk while working but now and again we would 'ha' foive minutes', as Jolt put it. This did not happen often as it wasn't tiring work, although we must have walked miles each day and Jolt rarely stopped. We would have a smoke and exchange a few words and, as usual, I had trouble understanding Jolt's accent. He always wore what he described as a slop and a ganzer. The latter was a dark wool jumper and over it he wore the former, which was a blue linen smock. He had a habit which both intrigued and disgusted me. He would blow his nose on to the ground, while holding it between two fingers. He liked to say that he threw away what the rich man kept in his pocket! I tried it myself once, with disastrous results.

During my time at the farm a sort of mutual respect grew between us. He was such a hard worker and knew so much about everything – horses, crops, weather, soil – that one had to admire him. I suppose he accepted me because I was happy to do anything that I was asked and never grumbled or questioned orders. After all, I was the newcomer and they had been doing it all their lives. My days in the Land Army were certainly good for me. Apart from learning a lot about farming and nature, it also taught me to be self-reliant and to work things out for myself. When you are in the middle of fields, miles from anybody and there is a problem, you just have to solve it on your own, or you are not much use.

Jolt's Norfolk accent completely defeated me one day. I was working in the yard when he rode in on one of the mares. He said something to me that sounded like Chinese: 'Ha' tin bum bin?' he said. It was obviously a question, but I couldn't answer it. He repeated the mysterious phrase somewhat sharply but I still looked at him blankly. Luckily Billy and Jimmy came into the yard just then and were able to explain to me. It seemed that they were expecting a visit from the Suffolk stallion to cover one of the mares and for some extraordinary reason the man in charge of this horse was known by the nickname of Tin Bum! Norfolk villages are great places for nicknames, some-times handed down from father to son, but I was a 'furriner' and couldn't be expected to know this. Just then, the missing Tin Bum rode into the yard on a magnificent horse and I was hastily despatched to a far distant field so that I should not see what went on in the yard and thus cause embarrassment to the men and to myself.

I caused some embarrassment when I took Tinker to the blacksmith in the village. A modest man, he worked only with farm horses, as there were no riding horses in the area, and never before had a horse come to his forge accompanied by a woman. It wouldn't have been so bad if Tinker hadn't obviously been scared stiff by the whole business; he must have been frightened by some past incident. Anyway his nerves seemed to affect his bladder and his bowels. I grabbed a pail and hastily held it under each orifice in turn, otherwise the floor would have become dangerously slippery. The blacksmith's face was crimson, but I'm afraid that I got an attack of the giggles.

Sometimes I was very privileged to take the horses to marsh at the end of a day's work. Judy and Blossom walked together with me sitting on one of them and Tinker followed behind. The problem for me was getting onto my chosen steed. I would put her alongside a five-barred gate, climb up the gate and clamber across onto her back to sit sideways on. She was much too large to ride crossways. Every time I reached the top bar of the gate, the wretched animal would take one step sideways so that I couldn't get on. Down I would come and put her back again but the same thing would happen. I learned to leap, bottom first, across the gap. Once up there, it was lovely. We would move off and I could feel her warmth and sniff the nice smell of horse. We ambled down the lanes, me singing at the top of my voice a popular song of the day. I would let them into the marsh, where they cantered around happily.

I Buy a Boat

THE carpenter who had made our wheelbarrow had built a very nice rowing boat. It was long with a transom stern. If it had a type name, I never knew it, but it was much longer and narrower than a dinghy. I don't remember what it cost, but it couldn't have been very expensive, and anyway, there was nothing else to spend my money on in those days. I could not buy clothes without coupons and I seldom went near any shops or towns. I didn't need new or smart clothes with the life that I led. Babe and I used to sometimes wear each other's dresses for a change.

I bought the boat, and, like the wheelbarrow, I had somehow to get it to Ludham. Neatishead was quite a way by road, but it was even further going round by the rivers. I got in touch with my friend Ann, who was still working at Hoveton, and we spent a weekend rowing it home. We biked to Neatishead on Saturday, put our bikes into the boat and set off across Barton Broad and down the river Ant. We saw no one all the way and it was so peaceful with wild-fowl everywhere: ducks, coots, grebes and herons. It was not unusual to see a bittern in those days.

On Saturday evening we moored our craft at St

Benet's Abbey ruins on the river Bure, by those same marshes where the cows and the three horses were grazing. We obeyed the law and hid the oars somewhere in the reeds at a distance, to prevent an enemy paratrooper using the boat if he should happen to drop nearby! We biked a mile or so across the causeway to Ludham and Hillview, where Ann stayed the night with us. It was lovely to see her again and to talk about our friends and the farms.

We got up early the next day and biked down to the Abbey, found the oars, loaded our bikes and rowed along the Bure until we turned into Thurne river, passing windmills, and eventually up Womack Dyke, almost to Ludham village, then into a small dyke to Hall Common Farm, where my boat was going to be kept, by permission of Mr Richies. We put the oars and rowlocks into a shed in the yard, in case that paratrooper was still lurking.

I enjoyed my boat in my spare time, just rowing along the river and the reedy dykes and watching birds. Sometimes I took the Richies' young daughter out for a trip. She was a very nice girl. I had called my boat Takali, which was the name of the airfield in Malta where Scottie had been stationed. I painted the name onto the stern.

During the summer Scottie had leave and he came to Norfolk to see me, his squadron having moved from Ludham some time previously. This coincided with a visit from a dear schoolfriend of mine, Joy, who had come with her husband and two friends for a short holiday. Joy worked in a factory making aeroplanes. I asked for a week off work and we all went to stay at Sutton Staithe. We had a lovely time, each glad to have a respite from work or war, just pottering about and relaxing. We went to the nearby beach, though some of it was still mined and covered with anti-invasion obstacles. A part must have been cleared, for I have a photograph of us sitting on the sand. The threat of invasion was passing now; the Germans had not been able to invade us in 1940, and now that we were much better armed and prepared for them, they were less likely to try it. We had my boat with us on the river near the Staithe and we rowed around among the water lilies and sometimes the boys went fishing in it. I don't remember if they ever caught anything.

We were happy enough together and yet, somehow, our romance was beginning to fade a little. Wartime conditions did not help at all. Long enforced absences were the cause of many couples and many marriages breaking up, and there were always plenty of others, lonely themselves, who were ready to console the other lonely ones.

It was now 1943 and the war had been going on for almost four years. It was to last another two years, but of course, we couldn't know this. The following year,

1944, was the year that the Allies were ready at last to invade Europe. It is all history now: D-day, 6 June, when the armies of Britain, America and Canada sailed across the channel to invade the Normandy beaches, with a small army of free Frenchmen.

The first that we at home knew about this was when it was announced on the radio that very morning. Everybody rushed to spread the news. I must have heard it on the farm, for the Richies listened to the news every day, like everyone else. We all knew someone who must have gone with the invading forces, and the next days were lived in a mixture of pride and dread. A land girl friend of mine heard that her fiancé had been killed on the first day.

All through the war I wrote down the names of friends who were killed. I wrote them inside the end pages of my prayer book. By the end of the war there were twenty-seven names of young men that I had known. One was my cousin who had been killed flying in Egypt. Two that I added at the end of the war were young French friends who had been in the Resistance and who were shot by the Germans. They were both just nineteen years old.

Meanwhile, on the farm, work continued and the seasons came and went with their various different jobs and I became a bit more skilful at some of them. I did enjoy it, even the hard bits, like the mornings when it was so frosty that metal tools stuck to the hands.

A bright spot was when a girlfriend asked me if I would like to go with her on a special outing. Jeanne worked in her father's boatyard. In peacetime they built motor cruisers for the Broads holidaymakers. Now they were making fast sea-going boats for the Air-Sea Rescue work. Jeanne had worked her way up, starting from literally knocking in nails to being in charge of all the equipment for these craft.

A finished boat was due to go to sea on trial, which consisted, among other things, of sailing at full speed up and down a measured mile off the coast near Lowestoft. Jeanne had been invited to go with them, as she had worked on the boat, and to bring a friend if she wished, so that she would not be the only woman on board. My Guv'nor gave me a half day off and I wore my Land Army uniform, for lack of anything else suitable.

It really was exciting! We belted up and down the coast at a terrific speed. It was a beautiful day, blue sky and blue sea and white spray and wash behind us.

I was invited to climb into a gun turret, of which there were at least two, one on each side. Although she was a rescue ship, she had to be armed against attack. The turret was a small circular perspex construction with just enough room for a gun and a seat. I sat on this and peered through the gun sights. Just then some joker began to spin the turret. With the motion of the sea and now this giddy spinning, I got out fast, afraid of disgracing myself.

A much larger ship steamed past our vessel. They sent us a signal: 'We see you have the Land Army on board' which caused some amusement. It was really a marvellous experience and another privilege for me as civilians were seldom allowed on board military craft.

It must seem as if I was often on holiday or having time off. This was not the case at all, for in over five years in the Land Army I had one week off a year and odd days or half-days now and again. But these were often the highlights of my life and I remember them clearly.

The Harvest and Threshing

THE first harvest of the year was in June; cutting and stacking the hay was then known by its old name of the 'haysel'. Hay was animal food for the winter, plants like clover, lucerne and vetches. It was often sown under another crop, so that when that crop was harvested, the hay would continue to grow. Hay had to be dry and rain at this time of year was a problem. It was left spread in the rows where it was cut and turned with rakes once or twice, depending on the weather. Tinker and I would gather it into long heaps with the horse-rake, which were then made into haycocks to dry completely. Then it was carted to be made into a neat sweet-smelling stack for the winter. When used, it was cut with an enormous knife with the handle at right angles. I never did manage to use this, so it was always Jolt's job and he cut neat blocks like slices of cake. Haystacks had to be checked frequently to see that they didn't heat up in the centre. Jolt did this with a long metal rod pushed in and then carefully felt for any sign of warmth which could have caused the stack to ignite.

The big event of the farming year was the corn harvest, which took place in late August and September. It is a curious fact that the dates of school holidays are still based on the agricultural calendar of long ago. It was accepted then that women and children were needed to help with certain farm work, and so the autumn term still begins at the end of harvest time.

During the war years the harvesting was done as it had always been done in the old days. I am so lucky to have seen this. We did use a binder, whereas the corn had previously been cut by men with scythes. A binder was a machine, pulled by two horses, or by tractor, which cut the stalks at ground level and by means of revolving 'sails' laid them flat onto an endless band which conveyed them into an intricate system of string and levers which tied the corn neatly into sheaves and pushed them out onto the field. It rattled and it was dusty. Jolt sat on a seat up behind the horses and they went round the field in an anti-clockwise direction in ever-diminishing circles. As Jolt was cutting, we others worked at standing up the sheaves in groups of about ten, propped up so that the air could circulate between them.

Even then, the men had to make the first cut round the outside of the field with scythes. This was to make room for the binder to get in next to the hedge for the first cut. In order to begin cutting in the mornings, the corn had to be dry and on some days there was a heavy dew. One morning the men and I stood in the cart shed, waiting for the order to begin. The Guv'nor, who never could make his mind up very quickly about anything, was pacing up and down in front of the shed. It was then that Roger the cowman made an immortal remark that I shall never forget; 'Blast,' he said. 'He don't know if he's fartin' or sneezin' if that weren't for the jar of his arse.' Jolt took charge and decided that the corn was dry enough to begin, which was what the Guv'nor was hoping for.

As the standing corn became smaller and smaller, all the rabbits became concentrated in the centre. Everyone in a village knew when a field was being cut and men with guns and boys with sticks would come to 'run rabbits' as the creatures made a dash for the hedge, and many a rabbit pie was made as a result.

The oats were the first corn to be cut. These were soft and pleasant to handle. Next came the barley, which had long sharp 'harns' on each grain which broke off and got into your socks or under your belt and were very uncomfortable, especially if you were hot and sweaty. Last to be cut was the wheat, with stiffer straw than the others, and the most important, as it provided bread for all.

We carted the corn in the old way. Blossom and Judy each pulled a large cart and one person on it would load it. This was quite difficult, as you had to 'keep your corners out' and build the sides up straight, otherwise it would all fall off or become pyramid-shaped. Two others would pitch the sheaves up to the cart with pitchforks. I was often on the cart, as it was slightly less hard work than pitching, but we were all pouring with sweat. Each time the horse had to move on, someone would 'haller hold-ye', which told the one on the cart to stick their fork in and hold on and which the horse understood to mean move on. As each cartload was finished it trundled slowly across the field, with the loader sitting on top, as it was too high to get off. We would draw up beside where Jolt was in charge of making the corn stack. Like the loads, this rose up beautifully straight with neat corners. When it was finished he would thatch it with last year's straw to keep the rain out, for the stacks stood for some time before the threshing engine could come during the winter.

Harvesting was pretty hard work and extra men were taken on to help, as there were only four of us when Roger was occupied with the cows. The very last load was brought to the stack with much rejoicing, but all the old customs had been lost there, nor did we have the traditional harvest supper. It would have been difficult with rationing.

Eventually the threshing engine would arrive. It was a steam engine with a funnel puffing out smoke and it rumbled along the roads, towing the big red threshing drum behind it and the elevator behind that. We knew when it was coming and more men were taken on as the whole operation needed quite a lot of labour.

The engine and the drum would be positioned beside the first stack to be threshed, with an endless belt between them to drive the machinery. The elevator would be positioned where the straw stack was to be. The stack was stripped of its thatch and the sheaves were pitched to the man on the drum, who skilfully cut the string and fanned the stalks out, ears first, into the machine. Inside the drum the grains were separated from the straw, and the corn came out of one hole into large sacks, hooked on to receive it. The straw emerged on to the elevator and fell on to the straw stack, where men arranged it tidily. All the residue, the chaff and bits of muck − known as the 'colder' − came to me. As I was the 'boy' on the farm, I had the dirtiest job, which was to remove the sacks of colder as they filled and carry them away. They were large but very light for their size. The entire operation was very dusty, but my bit was especially so. I had a scarf tied over my head, string tied round my legs to prevent mice running up my trousers, and the corners of my eyes were full of black muck. Not a pretty sight.

The good thing on threshing days was that we always finished early. One stack a day would last us till about half-past three, then we could go home. I would get straight into the bath and drink lots of tea. We were lucky, as few houses in the countryside had a bathroom in those days.

Victory at Last

THE war in Europe finally came to an end on 8 May 1945. The war against Japan in the Far East went on until August, still being hard fought by the Americans and the British over a vast area of land and sea.

In Britain there was tremendous rejoicing and celebrating, with dancing in the streets and parties for the children and pubs overflowing. That evening I biked to Sutton Staithe. I realised a bit sadly that it was perhaps an omen for the future that I went there on my own. Scottie was miles away and there was no particular friend around to accompany me. However, once arrived at the Staithe, the bar was full of people that I knew, both locals and Air Force, and we all spent a cheerful and happy evening celebrating.

Apart from the fact that peace meant the end of hostilities – fighting, bombing and killing – the end of the war didn't change much in our daily life. It would take a very long time for all the soldiers, sailors and airmen to return to civilian life and for factories to change back to their peacetime activities from making aeroplanes, tanks and weapons. The Land Army girls were needed to continue work on the farms until most of the men returned. It was finally disbanded in 1952.

I have no idea of when I stopped being a farm labourer and left the Land Army. I didn't keep a diary and dates are easily forgotten, but I think that I continued until early 1946. I do know that, alone amongst all the services, the WLA was the only one whose members did not receive the grant of money – known as a gratuity – to help us back into civilian life. There was quite an uproar about this: everyone thought it was most unfair and later King George VI said to Lady Denman, the WLA Director, 'We always thought that the land girls were not well treated.'

I have since read in books about the Land Army that all the girls had a personal letter from the Queen, who was our Patron, thanking them for all their hard work, but I never received this. Nor had I ever seen, or even heard about, a magazine for the Land Army, which was published throughout the war. I must have been too remote in my little corner of Norfolk. We had to hand in our uniforms, which I grudged, especially my well-worn leather boots. So I have nothing to show for my five years' work, except a couple of badges, good muscles and splendid health.

Before I left Hall Common Farm the Guv'nor asked me if I would give a few lessons to my successor. This was a young man from the village who was very deaf. He perched on the footplate beside me, while we drove around the fields and I showed him how the various implements worked, pointing to things and making gestures. After a short time he was able to take over from me.

Eventually petrol came off the ration and I could drive our car again and I didn't have to take a driving test. All who had a provisional licence before the war and who had driven throughout the war, whether lorries, jeeps, tractors or tanks, were excused the test. We had learned to drive the hard way!

Personally I felt a bit lost after the war ended. I now realise, from reading books about that time, that many other people felt the same sense of anticlimax as I did. One had the impression that although we were still very young, that the best part of our life was over, especially those who had been in the worst of the fighting and in the great battles in which they had been regarded as heroes – which indeed they were. Now they returned to a rather dreary civilian life, wearing a 'de-mob' suit, given to them with the gratuity, to tide them over until they could return to a pre-war job. But so many had joined up at eighteen years old, that they had no job to return to and found themselves among thousands of others who were unemployed and forced to look for work.

It didn't help that the whole country was in a state of exhaustion after such an enormous effort and heavily in debt to America. Everything was in short supply for a long time after the war, and even bread was rationed for the first time. Clothes were still rationed when I was married in 1948. I didn't marry Scottie. We met for the last time in 1946, so at least I knew that he survived the war.

Oddly enough I was to spend twenty years of my life in a house on Hall Common Farm. It was originally three small thatched cottages and almost derelict when we bought them. They stood in the midst of the fields where I had worked and with the far views across the marshes, and the gentle ghosts of three plodding horses.

I was glad to have known farming as it used to be since time immemorial. There were to be great changes in agriculture and so many things were to vanish for ever. Not only old implements and ways of working, but many birds, wild flowers and wildlife would also vanish by the end of the century. Combine harvesters were soon to come into use, which could do the entire corn harvest with just one machine, two men and a lorry. There would be no more carefully made stacks, no horses and carts, no one to 'haller hold-ye' any more and no dusty days of threshing. Pesticides and poisons were to arrive and farmyard muck to be replaced with stronger and more polluting fertilisers.

It had been such a good life, I had learnt such a lot and I wouldn't have missed it for anything.

I'd better go and cook those carrots for lunch now.

About the Author

JOAN Snelling was born in London in 1922.

She joined the Women's Land Army in Norfolk during the Second World War and continued to live in the same village for a further thirty years.

In 1975 she and her husband moved to France. He had been badly injured and burned in a wartime bomber crash and died in 1986.

Today she still lives in the same hamlet in a rural area where she is well known as a water colour painter.

Other Titles from Old Pond Publishing

Land Girls at the Old Rectory IRENE GRIMWOOD
Light–hearted, boisterous memories of land girls in Suffolk 1942–46. Paperback.

Early to Rise HUGH BARRETT
A classic of rural literature, this is an honest account of a young man working as a farm pupil in Suffolk in the 1930s. Paperback.

A Good Living HUGH BARRETT
Following on from *Early to Rise*, Hugh takes us back to the assortment of farms with which he was involved from 1937 to 1949. Paperback.

Chaffinch's H W FREEMAN
H W Freeman's moving novel depicts the life of farm worker Joss Elvin and his struggle to raise a family on 19 acres of Suffolk farmland. Paperback.

Joseph and His Brethren H W FREEMAN
First published in 1928, this novel follows the story of a Suffolk farming family through two generations. Paperback.

Farmers' Films EAST ANGLIAN FILM ARCHIVE
A programme of six short films mostly from the 1950s, shot by farmers on their own farms. Locations include Essex, Suffolk, Norfolk and Cambridgeshire. The emphasis is on field operations.

In a Long Day DAVID KINDRED AND ROGER SMITH
Two hundred captioned photographs of farm work and village life in Suffolk 1925–33. Paperback.

Free complete catalogue:
Old Pond Publishing
Dencora Business Centre, 36 White House Road,
Ipswich IPI 5LT, United Kingdom.
Phone: 01473 238200   Fax: 01473 238201
Website: www.oldpond.com   Email: enquiries@oldpond.com